AHA!

Bridge to New Possibilities

BARBARA CABALLERO

WESTBOW
PRESS®
A DIVISION OF THOMAS NELSON
& ZONDERVAN

WestBow Press books may be ordered through booksellers or by contacting:

WestBow Press
A Division of Thomas Nelson & Zondervan
1663 Liberty Drive
Bloomington, IN 47403
www.westbowpress.com
844-714-3454

ISBN: 978-1-6642-0435-5 (sc)
ISBN: 978-1-6642-0434-8 (e)

Print information available on the last page.

WestBow Press rev. date: 10/05/2020

INTRODUCTION

You may have read "Everything I Need to Know I Learned in Kindergarten" or "Everything I Need to Know I Learned from the Golden Books." But I would propose that everything I need to know I learned along the way. In our very first days we learn the value of a smile. We learn how to laugh. No better lesson will produce so much good in our lives and in the world. It is the first way that we make a difference.

Knowing that a smile makes a difference does nothing unless you actually smile. So the question becomes how we get from knowledge to action. I propose we do this with a plan. I call these mini-plans "mental models". They remind us to use the wonderful things we have learned along the way like looking both ways before you cross the street. There are so many streets you will cross in your life. Wouldn't it be nice if some of the things we choose to do just sort of came naturally?

The suggestions in this book are about models I have made from discoveries along the way. I offer them as possibilities to emulate and as ideas for building your own "mental models". Enjoy!

SHARING OUR STORIES

Every story told carries branches of meaning.
I have built my mental models
To help guide my choices,
From the stories I have read or heard
Or seen played out.
We gather meaning through relationships.
We are called to work
With what we are given.
Our task is to listen
For the story, insights, even questions,
To seek our next teachers.
We see only fragments,
Rough cut gems, and
Work to understand their meaning.

Contents

BEGINNINGS

Make it A Great Day

Long ago I read that the Arabians do not say "Have a great day", but rather "Make it a great day", believing that it was up to them to make it so. I liked that and took it on as my motto. So I frequently say to others "Make it a great day" usually as I end any conversation or interaction.

Throughout the day I pause and wonder how can I make this a great day? What can I say or do that will make a difference? What opportunities are there that I might take on? Who needs a listening ear or a helping hand?

When my eldest daughter was a toddler, I was dropping my husband off for work one day and she said "Make great day Daddy." It was her first sentence and I was thrilled.

So, this is what I think to myself as I open my eyes each day. It is also how I look back at the end of the day to what has transpired.

"Yes, this has been a great day!"

Hour of Power

Stephen R. Covey taught us to use "the hour of power". He would have us start every day with four areas: spiritual, social, mental and physical. He recommends starting with prayer (in whatever way that means to you). I ask my Heavenly Father what I need to do, be and learn. And then I listen. I seem to hear better when I am writing, so I journal. I keep a separate journal to record what I receive as I listen and ponder.

Julia Cameron calls this "morning pages" and writes whatever comes as fast as she can for ten minutes or three full pages. Sometimes this releases the "should a's" and the worries. Whatever comes, getting it out and on paper helps us to let it go. Then we can prioritize and get on with whatever is important.

Others use meditation to center and tune into the day.

The specific technique does not seem as important as the idea of getting in tune with whatever you believe and whatever guidance you choose to accept.

For the mental realm, Robin Sharma tells us that 10,000 hours will make us a genius in whatever field we choose, so spend at least a half hour reading something you want to know more about.

The physical is stretching and exercise. It may be walking, running, biking or even a gym program. It might be yoga or Tai chi. The important thing is to keep a regular schedule. This also involves eating well and moderately.

Finally, we are ready to reach out to others, to appreciate, to share and to make a difference.

The specific way you approach each area is not important. Build your own mental model. Try one thing and then another. Find out what works for you and establish a routine so that doing this comes naturally.

Once your routine is solid and working for you, occasionally make an alteration and see if that works better. Keep experimenting and perfecting this and every other mental model.

"To Do" Lists

I have made lists all of my life, and graphs, and mind maps. They probably come from a goal list mentality. But, I also love tracking what I have accomplished. So I have devised a new kind of "to do" list that works well for me. I divide my page into four columns. The first is my "to do" list, the second and third are for what I have done and the last is for the items I have taken time to savor. I need this list, because my driven attitude makes it hard to stop at a threshold (an interval between tasks) and pause to be pleased with accomplishments instead of just crossing them off.

I have, over the years, added other columns and even taken columns away, but this seems to work best for me. It feels good to realize that even when half of my "to do" list remains undone; I have been adaptable and met the needs before me and even enjoyed the process.

So, I recommend being creative about the "how" of getting things done. Find out what works best for you. Be ready and willing to experiment with other ideas as you come across them. Make it all a marvelous adventure.

Setting an Intent

I do not know where I first came across the idea of setting an intent for the day. Perhaps it came from the importance of goal setting or the need to prioritize. Wherever it came from, it is a part of the way that I start every day. I spend some time with a good book and with my meditation and listen for the idea that will form my intent for the day.

I write that intent down in my journal and perhaps I even spend some time journaling on what it means to me. The more ways I can get the idea out there, the more likely I am to remember it throughout the day and bring myself back to the center it provides.

I look at my vision for the day, my plans and priorities and see how it will augment all I mean to do.

I write it on post-it notes and put it on my mirror, on the front door, above my kitchen sink, any place I know I will be spending time. I put it on the dashboard of the car.

Whenever I move from task to task, I think about it.

In the evening I look back to see how it has made a difference and what I have learned.

You can also set intents for longer periods if you like: a week, a month. If I set an intent for a year I may call it a motto to live by.

ATTITUDE

Random Acts of Kindness

From my mother's knee, I learned to be helpful, to make friends by being nice, by being friendly to the girl sitting alone or feeling sad. There was once a girl in elementary school that I did not like. When she got sick, I sent her a get well card, just to let her know I was nicer than she was. In a way, that backfired. She was so appreciative that when she came back to school she looked me up, thanked me and we became best friends.

These days I notice that my children, also, are naturally helpful to others. One daughter got married before she was out of high school. But she has spent her life helping others. She started working in a childcare center, learned early childhood education, and has her own handicapped children that she has loved, cared for and made a difference for. They are all grown and doing well. Now she is an elder-care-giver, working in a group home giving people the opportunity to be as independent as they are able and providing the support and encouragement they need.

I used to be concerned about panhandlers and would avoid areas where they were known to hang out. Then I decided I could provide a meal or socks or fruit, without giving money. At last, I learned to give up judgment and just help where I could. My task is to give as I am able and let the choices they make be their choices and not my concern.

Another important area of giving is with our presence, our

listening. In grief, what a person needs most is someone around them. I let them lead any conversation and am just present.

As with most of us, if you asked me what I am here for, I would say to make a difference. This naturally expands into the idea of "pay it forward" – doing something nice for someone and suggesting that they pay it forward.

The movie, "Pay It Forward", took this to a new level for me. In it, the ten year old lead is taught in school to do something for three people that they could not do for themselves. The movie suggests that connections, that we never know, will occur.

Consider your own ideas about kindness and sharing. What do you love to do? How can you make a difference? Decide on a mental model that works for you in this realm and enjoy the results.

Response - Ability

S omeone says something and you can feel the anger rise up in your throat-the retort that will smash him once and for all. But wait! Stephen R. Covey said that we should put a pause between his words and our response. We have the ability to pause and consider: the intent, the circumstances, the alternatives, and the best course of action. He called this response – ability, taking responsibility for our response.

This mental model has many times quieted the embers of an eruption and made it possible to maintain peace. In fact this is my favorite conflict resolution technique. My parents called this counting to ten. But it is more than that. It is more related to the idea of witnessing, stepping back and seeing the situation from a more distant perspective.

It also relates to the old saw, "would you rather be right or in harmony?" In the instant we all might say, "but, I am right". Upon consideration we might really prefer harmony. Then perhaps we can come back at another time and talk about what we heard, what we felt, and what we want or need.

Think about how, when, or if you might use this mental model and what the results might be. Is this an idea worth a try in the life you are leading today? Might it make a difference?

Thresholds

We all tend to put in very full days moving quickly from one activity to another. There is always more to do. Prioritizing helps and tackling the hard one first.

But there is another way too. I have learned to use thresholds to break apart my tasks. When I move from work preparations to heading out the door, I like to pause for just a moment and honor where I have been and where I am going. A doorway makes a lovely threshold reminder. Pause, breathe, and smile.

A cup of coffee or tea is another way to take a pause and consider. Friends provide a refreshing pause, and an interlude of enjoyment.

Authorities suggest that if you pause every 60-90 minutes from an intense task and just go for a short walk, you are providing another sort of energy restoring pause. This also allows your unconscious mind to work for you.

When I finish my work day and arrive home, I like to pause, change clothes and sit down with a cup of tea and a good book that is suited to short reads and a bit of pondering. Then I am ready for the needed home activities.

You can also allow your children to provide a pause, refreshment, as you listen to them tell about their day. If you are a stay-at-home Mom, you might have a drink and hot cookies waiting for your children.

Perhaps after everyone is tucked in bed, your last threshold pause of the day might be a look back at the day and its successes and releasing all that did not go as well as expected.

Give Up Littleness

I was raised to respect my elders, to be polite and quiet, and to consider others first.

I was taught that if I go to a restaurant with someone, I should order something on the low-priced portion of the menu.

So, I have always been "low maintenance" – willing to go along, to let others choose, to require little, to be kind, courteous and thoughtful.

I preferred to let someone else decide where we would go and what we would do.

I had just walked away from a dinner group to make way for another when I came across a book that changed my perspective. Joan Borysenko teaches that we should give up "littleness". "Littleness" says everyone is more important than I am; that I do not need a voice. That what I offer is less important.

I am learning to be inclusive, but not to think myself less than others.

I love group activities, especially small groups where we can share and hear each other. I am learning to listen, to ask questions, to wonder and to share. I am learning to speak from my heart and to share my truths and consider others' truths.

In finding our similarities, our common ground we grow closer and expand what we know and what we believe.

Nuggets and Chaff

Several years ago I made a long drive to attend a conference. In the process I came down with a cold. So, I was definitely not feeling my best. The conference was expensive and was held at a lovely resort.

My first major disappointment was that the speaker was detained and did not show for the first evening session. The group went forth and put together a nice congenial evening, but that was not what I had come for.

The program was held as planned on Saturday. Then we learned that our speaker had another conflicting appointment and would leave that night and not be there for the Sunday closing session. I was not happy. These many years later I do not even remember what the topic was.

But I distinctly remember the speaker who led the meditation that next morning and said that we should listen well, take in what was important, the nuggets for the sessions and blow the rest away as so much chaff. I was impressed with this idea. I am still impressed.

Now as I complete a conference or a lecture or a meeting, I take time to look back and pick out the nuggets, the gold that rang true for me in what I heard. And I do let the rest go.

This has become another of my mental models. I love putting a positive aspect on the time and savoring its goodness. I love thinking about how I will put what I have learned to use in my life, thinking of how it makes a difference.

So I have expanded this to look back at each day and extract the goodness and spend a few minutes savoring the best of the day.

Stand in Your Power

Even when we have accomplished something, we tend to denigrate the task, make it seem little and unimportant, or once accomplished we feel the need to go on to the next item on our "to do" list. The mental model a friend introduced me to for this is "stand in your power".

Take the time to savor your accomplishment, to feel good about it. Share it with others and listen to what they say. Take it in fully. Smile. Breathe. Listen. Enjoy.

My church once set up a book signing for me when I completed and published a book of poetry. People brought in refreshments. I stood in the back of the room, making space for the people to come in, look at the book and pick up some refreshments. A great friend told me to step forward, to reach out to people, to shake their hands, to welcome them. Stand for who you are. Be a leader, an example, a teacher.

That was such great advice, I have always remembered it. And so now I continue to accomplish, but I take the time to savor my accomplishments, to share them, and to encourage others to go forward and accomplish as well.

As an example, I keep a library of books by local authors, read them, get them autographed, and share my positive thoughts with the authors.

We are all creative and need to share our successes. We can do more with the encouragement of each other.

So try this on. Stand for who you are and be a leader in what you do. You can make it a great day!

Synchronicities

Synchronicity is like a pointer saying pay attention to this. It might happen when you are attracted to a specific book or when the same topic comes up over and over in your daily activities. Something concrete happens and your intuition says "Yes". A meaning comes to you. A new depth. A new perspective.

James Redfield says expect synchronicities. Be open to the possibilities they offer. Give them your attention.

The first step is to be aware of your intuition; to listen to those tiny proddings that come from within.

It was Carl Jung who first came up with the concept.

Jean Shinoda Bolen proposes an Agatha Christie approach to our synchronicities:

What is the meaning of this event?

What are the circumstances in which it arose?

What are the possibilities inherent in it?

Authors who talk about it include: Carl Jung, Richard Eyre, Jean Shinoda Bolen, and James Redfield.

Much here is based on belief. If you are open to these ideas, they will come to you and the possibilities are rich. If you are of a more linear mindset and demand proof, you will not be likely to see or recognize synchronicity.

If these ideas interest you find time to read more, to experiment with them, to take on what works for you.

Laughter Therapy

I have always loved laughing with my friends, but I began to notice that I do not find a lot of jokes funny. People tell me I am too serious. So I started researching what I find funny. I like stories that show people being vulnerable, making mistakes and learning from them. I like looking back at things that have happened and seeing the humor in them after the fact, things that were not at all funny at the time.

Then I saw an announcement for a Laughter Therapy Weekend Retreat and decided this was just the thing for me. The speaker was a "Doctor". She started by opening her mouth wide, throwing her head back and laughing long and loud. We all fidgeted in our chairs wondering if she was laughing at one of us. But "No" she said, she was just enjoying the pleasure of hearty laughter. She invited all of us to laugh. We found it disconcerting. But we were there to learn, so we gave it a half-hearted attempt. We sounded funny and soon we were laughing in sheer glee. It was a great weekend.

She told us that children play with their problems. We need to do the same. To contemplate laughing at our problems was enough to shift our attitude.

Make it a goal to enjoy every moment. Practice whole-hearted laughter. She taught us to "fake it until you make it". You can even start with a simple "tee he".

Asking "why" stops the flow of laughter. Just go with it. Express your feelings directly.

Now there are laughter yoga classes that promote enjoying our laughter.

A word of caution: teasing, satire and ridicule are not producers of happiness. Make your laughter a pleasure, not an attack on another.

We are told we need a certain number of laughs each day. Can you find out how many that is?

To Have or Not Have

We all have desires, things we want. Little things like an ice cream cone and big things like a dependable car. But the hardest things to want are often those we once had and some rule or new regulation or circumstance has taken away. Like a certain level of health care or access to a specific store. We don't seem to treasure what we have until it is taken away.

One year I had a bad case of bronchitis that kept me inside and down for more than six weeks. I could only take slow, shallow breaths. The day I was well enough to go outside and walk down to the mailbox felt like a miracle. It was like magic to be able to take a full deep breath. How I appreciated the ability to breathe.

Do you remember the love and concern we all felt for each other after 9/11 and our patriotism? It did not last long, but it was heartwarming while it did.

Many years ago I was in an area of drought and we were rationed on when we could water our lawns or plants and supposed to bathe only on certain days. That was when I went to church and heard a returned missionary talk about life in an African country he had been to where the only source of water was seven miles away and the women carried home the water they needed every morning in jars on their heads.

The point is we all need to be grateful for all we have and to count our blessings which usually start with the people in our lives.

Why do you suppose that the very poor in Bhutan were considered the happiest in the world a few years ago?

Some recommend that we write daily gratitude lists, but that gets old fast. Others recommend writing gratitude lists once a week. Still others of us spend some time pondering blessings in our morning meditations. Choose how you will remember to be grateful. Try out different routines until you find one that works for you. Change it periodically to keep it fresh and valuable. Be creative.

Even This Shall Pass Away

As a child, I knew that my Daddy loved poetry and so I would memorize his favorite poems to recite to him. One of these was "This Too Shall Pass".

> Once in Persia reigned a king,
> Who upon his signet ring
> Graved a maxim true and wise,
> Which, if held before his eyes,
> Gave him counsel at a glance
> Fit for every change and chance.
> Solemn words, and these are they;
> "Even this shall pass away."
>
> Trains of camels through the sand
> Brought him gems from Samarcand;
> Fleets of galleys through the seas
> Brought him pearls to match with these;
> But he counted not his gain
> Treasures of the mine or main;
> "What is wealth?" the king would say;
> "Even this shall pass away."

'Mid the revels of his court,
At the zenith of his sport,
When the palms of all his guests
Burned with clapping at his jests,
He, amid his figs and wine,
Cried, "O loving friends of mine;
Pleasures come, but do not stay;
'Even this shall pass away.'"

Lady, fairest ever seen,
Was the bride he crowned the queen.
Pillowed on his marriage bed,
Softly to his soul he said:
"Though no bridegroom ever pressed
Fairer bosom to his breast,
Mortal flesh must come to clay –
Even this shall pass away."

Fighting on a furious field,
Once a javelin pierced his shield;
Soldiers, with a loud lament,
Bore him bleeding to his tent.
Groaning from his tortured side,
"Pain is hard to bear," he cried;
"But with patience, day by day,
Even this shall pass away."

Towering in the public square,
Twenty cubits in the air,
Rose his statue, carved in stone.
Then the king, disguised, unknown,
Stood before his sculptured name,
Musing meekly: "What is fame?
Fame is but a slow decay;
Even this shall pass away."

Struck with palsy, sore and old,
Waiting at the Gates of Gold,
Said he with his dying breath,
"Life is done, but what is Death?"
Then, in answer to the king,
Fell a sunbeam on his ring,
Showing by a heavenly ray,
"Even this shall pass away."

–Theodore Tilton

And so I was taught at an early age to accept what is and know that it will pass away if I am patient. This might have been Daddy's motto for his life. It certainly influenced mine.

Perhaps this will also help you to overcome and to be more patient. Think upon it.

RELATIONSHIPS

Mastermind Groups

I first came across this idea from Barbara Sher. She wrote of "Teamworks". This is a small group of like-minded folk that get together once a week. We share the week's successes. Then the new week's plans, and finally any problems or things we need help with. It is marvelous what this sense of accountability does for us. Knowing we will report our progress motivates us to do more, to stay on track. We all love to feel heard, supported, and encouraged. It lifts us, renews our energy, and prepares us to go forth in a good spirit.

Others have called this group a "kitchen cabinet", that group of special people brought together to help you further your goals.

Another form is called a "Mastermind Group". They use a 12 step process to augment the same material. Whatever you call it, whatever process you use, it motivates and challenges you to be more, to do more and to help others do more. It provides a path toward our own unlimited potential.

It's All in the Attitude

S ometimes a romance starts to sour when you start looking at what is wrong. We are taught to be careful, to consider the downsides of each other, to be wary of commitments. But, the more you start counting the little things that irritate, the deeper you drop into uncertainty.

One day I was recounting to a friend all the ways that my relationship was not perfect, when this very wise friend said, "It is all in the attitude." If you fear you are enabling a relationship, first try turning it all around and count the things he does right. What is good about this person? What really matters? I felt like I had been hit up the side of the head. What she said really clicked. I could choose to count the blessings, instead of the peccadillos.

Amazing the difference it made. I actually did a 180 turn in that relationship, allowed the happiness to grow and after a long engagement married him. We fit together nicely and know where and when to be dependent and independent. It all works.

This is rather like what we read about deciding what we want, seeing it as being present and then doing what we would be doing if it were present. This is sometimes called visioning or manifesting.

Perhaps it is all in the perspective. What do I choose to see?

When I am upset, I have learned to step back, to go quiet, to feel my feelings without expressing them and to move into a witness perspective where I see the bigger picture. I wonder what the other person sees and wants. I wonder how I would like to see the issue resolved and if I have the time and willingness to learn and listen, to be patient with another and with myself.

Make no mistake. This is difficult and takes a lot of practice. But the world also gives us many opportunities to practice. We try, we step back, we look beyond and we forgive ourselves again and again.

So perhaps the mental model is: pause, get quiet, consider, question, reflect, accept, resolve, forgive, and choose a wider perspective. Does it make a difference?

Pause

As a child, when I got scolded and stomped off, I would sometimes go for a long walk. I liked winding up at the, always open, chapel on the side of our church. I would go in there and sit and feel the reverence and look at the stained glass windows. When I had calmed down I would walk back home.

Yes, I probably did some crying and stomping and even talking back (not allowed at home), but I also had time to think, to let go, to count my blessings.

So, the message I took away from this was the ability to pause, feel my feelings and release them, then choose the next best step.

It is hard to stop when what you really want to do is bite his head off for whatever the offense you instantly felt. But it really works. Keep practicing "the step back and observe" stance.

I have also learned to love being out in nature or in a quiet, reverent place. Where do you like to go to reflect and thereby gain a wider perspective?

Loving Spoons

The quote we have all heard is "do unto others as you would have them do unto you." I grew up in a home where this was the way things were. I was taught to be thoughtful, to consider others needs first, and to respect my elders, which usually meant maintaining silence and listening well.

I was taught to wonder what others wanted, to put myself in their place and as much as I could provide what I would want. The problem with this perspective is that we are all different and our wants and needs are different.

If I would consider help in the kitchen a loving act, that does not mean that helping my husband do something he loves would be considered a loving act in his eyes. His favorite way of receiving love might be a homemade card which expresses specific ways I feel love and appreciate him.

So the new version of "Do unto others…" might be "Do unto others as they would have you do unto them." And part of the process then would include learning what says love to them. What is their language of love?

We learn that some of us learn best by seeing, others by hearing and still others need to actually get their hands in and touch,

This may also include public displays or a quiet personal approach.

All of this is learned over time within a relationship. I have hung a wooden spoon on my wall to remind me that we need to understand each other and do what we do in ways that appeal to the other. We need to figure out how we best fit together.

So I appreciate and respect him, while he helps me with my projects and we both feel loved and blessed to be together.

How does your best friend like to feel loved? How can you learn more about what he or she wants and provide more love

Acceptance

I have a favorite mantra: attend, acknowledge, accept, appreciate, act. It reminds me to take time to be present to the moment, to look around and notice. A part of noticing is acknowledging, taking the time to take in what I have noticed. Then comes the challenge of accepting what is, whether it is what I had hoped for or not. With an understanding of what is, I can move on. I can find meaning. I can find the goodness in what is. I can see possibilities. Only then am I able to decide on a mini-goal and a first step forward.

"Accepting what is" keeps me in the present, so that I can let the past be and not worry about what might happen. Accepting improves my ability to notice. Sometimes I take a pencil and sit outside and draw what I see. I draw only for myself and the ability to see more closely, whether it is a tiny flower I might otherwise overlook or even a pattern on a tree trunk, or the way a cloud moves.

Acceptance extends to the people with whom I come in contact. I am learning to accept them where they are. It does not seem to help to want them to be something else or do something else. It takes time to hear them, to be with them, to admire their path, their choices. Sometimes it takes a long walk in the forest, to ruminate and dwell in the pleasures of the moment: a breeze, a ray of sunshine, a bird song, a bit of reflection.

Aha!

LEARNING

Learning Cycles

When a new topic of interest comes up, I start by doing a little research, trying to get some basic facts. Then I talk to someone I trust and see what ideas, what information they may also have. Luckily, I belong to several groups that like to talk about the things I often ponder, so I take my new subject to them and get more ideas, more perspectives.

Having gathered these ideas I retreat to a place of reflection to ponder, to wonder, to probe. I write out what I have learned, what I now believe; then I take it back to a group again for discussion.

This cycle helps me grow and expand ideas and see other perspectives. This all feels good and helps me get a better idea of what the subject is all about. Of course, I continue to do research in an effort to learn more.

Debt Free

N ow this is a hard one until you make a mental model of it. I was, luckily, taught that one should only go into debt for a house, a car or an education. That is probably because my parents lived through the Great Depression and suffered the consequences of those times.

We used to have layaway. Actually, we still often do, but rarely use it. Then if we really wanted something, we could put it on layaway and pay for it a bit at a time until it was paid for and we could retrieve it. Another idea that helps is to not buy anything when you first see it, but think on it for a few days and if you really want it, figure out how you can come up with the money to get it.

If you have credit cards, get rid of all except one for emergency use. And make sure that anything you charge on it can be paid off within 30 days. Until you have done this, you cannot imagine how good it feels to know you are not paying any interest on your card/s.

The next step is a savings plan that puts away 10% of all earnings. You will be so glad you did this when it comes time to retire. This, of course, only works if you leave the money in the account where you choose to save it. No borrowing.

Okay, but perhaps you already have credit card debt. Then the first step is, again, to get rid of all but one card and then start paying off the others as fast as possible. Start with the one with the highest interest rate and pay as much as you can each month until that is paid off. Then go to the next one. Be sure to celebrate with the paying off of each card.

When you are ready to own your own home, choose a small home. You will be just as happy and there will be less upkeep. Learn all the 'do-it-yourself' things that you can. Then trade knowledge with others and even tools and time. Keep learning.

Buy your car two years old and let others pay the upfront depreciation. Then keep up the maintenance and keep your car as long as you can. Resources tell us the average people keep cars eleven and one half years. If, after it is paid off, you continue to put the amount of the payment into a special account, you will have money for necessary repairs and for a large down payment when it is time to get another car.

Whenever you come upon extra money put it first on any debts you have.

Massive Open Online Courses

S everal years ago I learned about massive open online courses. They are college courses available free or at nominal cost online. They can be found on almost any topic. The idea is to listen to daily lectures, take quizzes, enter into discussions and perhaps take a final. At the end you add new knowledge to your repertoire. The courses are usually eight weeks long.

You can start a course, learn what you need and drop out if you wish. It might go in a different direction from what you expected or be at a different depth.

Some of these classes can even be put together to get a degree. So you do not necessarily have to go to college to get that degree you need to get ahead.

The real lesson here is that these options are continually expanding and changing and it is important to keep up with what is going on and the possibilities that will promote your lifelong learning.

Keep reading, keep searching, and keep up with current events in the education field.

Check out Coursera, Udacity, Edu, etc.

The "aha's" are ever present, ever expanding.

Apprenticeships

In years gone by, most people learned through apprenticeships. They learned printing working in a print shop. They learned carpentry in a woodworking shop. They learned farming on their parent's farm. Everyone had jobs to do. They even learned law in a lawyer's office.

These days we go off to school. We learn math, reading, science, history. But where are the skills we need to be self-reliant? Even the woodworking and sewing classes of yesteryear are mostly missing from our schools. Where do we learn about personal finance? Perhaps we learn some of this at home. Perhaps a scouting program provides some of this.

I think there should be more opportunities for young people to learn, to take on apprenticeships in areas that interest them: electricity, plumbing, carpentry, automotive, etc.

My brother grew up at Dad's side building things: models, rabbit hutches, forts, tree houses, kites, even an airplane. I have a model of that airplane in my house. He became a machinist and a carpenter and makes the most amazing things.

Choose a skill you would like to know more about, find a Youtube on the topic and learn. Then ask around to see if you can find a professional in that area who would like a helper. Be willing to take the time to do the mundane things: to sweep, pick up, go and get what is needed. Learn about the tools of the trade and their care.

Take on one apprenticeship after another. And become a possibility thinker. "I can."

TRAVELING

Traveling Hints

Did you ever pack up for a trip and discover on the way down the road that you had not packed an item that you will need? Of course, we all have. So I started making packing lists. When I am planning a trip, I look at the list and pack the things on the list that I think I will need. When I go out and find I still need something that I do not have, I pull a little notebook out of my purse and write it down. Then I add it to the list when I get back home.

I now have different packing lists for going to the beach, going camping, long distance travel, and even business trips. They really do help.

I tend to carry a large organizer purse as well. But that can get mighty heavy, so I have learned to keep a back-up bag in the car. This way, when I go someplace, I put what I will really need in the purse and put the rest in the back-up bag and lock it in the trunk of my car. In addition, when you are out in an uncertain surroundings, a heavy duty bag is a discouragement to a "would be" thief. He wants to take from an easy prey. Walk tall and determinedly. Don't use your cell phone or read while you walk. Always pay attention and enjoy what is going on around you.

When I lived in an area where I needed to be a bit more careful, the first thing I did was take a self-defense course, so I would know when and where to go and how to be less attractive to the would be thief. This is a good course of action for anyone.

"What Should I Not Miss?"

When I was younger I always seemed to be in a rush to get somewhere, even when I was going clear across the country. Now I like to take my time, discover, learn along the way. I have learned to plan shorter days.

If I am going by car, as I enter each new State, I plan to stop at the Welcome Center to see what I might find along the way. I like to get a new State map and mark my path as I travel. Most State maps have mile markers that help you tell where you are in relation to other places. It is enjoyable to study your map and see what special places it marks out for you – like waterfalls, covered bridges and monuments.

Then I tell the lady at the Welcome Center what kinds of things I like to see and ask for her recommendations. These people usually know and love the area they are in and can give you all kinds of wonderful ideas. And they are often the kindest, friendliest people you can imagine. Take some time to enjoy their company and to appreciate what they are doing.

I have learned to expand this question to others, to waitresses and other travelers, to gas station attendants, to students, and to strangers. To quote someone we all know and love "O the wonders you will see."

AAA Books have interesting descriptions, histories and lists of attractions for the towns you go through that you might want to take time for.

I also like to break my travel up with "geocaches." If you do not know what these are look up the website geocaching.com and learn. They are like tiny treasure hunts outdoors and provide exercise, new vistas and a break from the drive. These caches are almost always hidden in areas of particular beauty or historical significance. Have fun.

Traffic

I have developed a clever trick for avoiding the frustration of traffic and particularly of people who cut in front of you or rush to pass. I imagine that they have some kind of emergency and are rushing to someplace really important, perhaps even a life or death matter. Then I smile, bless them and wish them success in whatever they are trying to get to.

A variation of this is tailgaters. If someone is following too close, I slow down. If that does not get them to back off or go around, I find a place to pull off the road and let them go again blessing them on the journey. It works for me and I feel better. What do you think? It might be worth a try.

Packing Lists

I want to be prepared, to take what I will need when I travel, but not anything I will not need. Over time I have learned to make a travel list of items I will need. I have one for travel, another for camping, one for backpacking and even one for going to the beach.

Every time I get ready for a trip, I pull out the appropriate list and go down it as I pack. When I find on a trip that I need something more, I make a note and add it to the appropriate list or lists when I get back home.

The other side of this effort is learning to pack clothes that travel well and do not wrinkle and to plan for variability in weather by layering clothing items.

Over time I have learned to plan my wardrobe around two basic colors and make sure everything mixes and matches.

Sometimes it is better not to pack something if it can be purchased cheaply where you will be and does not need to take up luggage space. My goal is to be able to travel with one bag that can be carried on and one large purse/book bag/snack bag. Did you know you can take an empty water bottle through security and then fill it at a fountain inside the airport?

I have also learned to roll my clothing items. They seem to fit better.

Think about the techniques you use when packing. Ask others for their best ideas. Build a plan and change it as you learn.

BOOKS/JOURNALS

A New Mental Model for Reading Books

When you first pick up a new book, perhaps a title that sounds attractive in the bookstore, how do you decide whether you want to read it? Are you attracted by the title or the author or the cover? My first version was to pick it up, read the first paragraph, then turn to page 66 and read another paragraph.

It used to be that that was about all you could do. Bookstore owners did not want you reading; there were no comfortable chairs, no tables, no café offering a cup of coffee and perhaps a pastry. But, a few stores changed and this offering was so loved by customers that it became more and more common.

Back to the book; if both of these paragraphs attracted me, it would go with me to a quiet place for further perusal.

These days I am doing more. Other writers have taught me to read the book ends, the publisher's words, and the introduction. Then I look at the table of contents to see where the book intends to take me and how it will address the journey.

Next, I go to the index, if there is one, and pick three topics of interest and check them to see what the author has to say about them.

This is the decision point. Now I am ready to buy the book. Back home I like to make a note of what attracted me and why I decided that I wanted to read the book.

I read a book with a highlighter and a pen in hand. The highlighter marks passages I particularly like and the pen makes notes, questions, agrees, and suggests further research. Often I will stop reading to ponder an idea and to write my thoughts about it and perhaps my experiences along the same lines.

When I finish the book, I copy all of the highlights into a book journal. Finally, I prioritize all I have highlighted and pick out the three most important ideas I have gained. These three ideas go on a 3x5 card for easy reference. I try to incorporate them into my life in some way. I give them extra time and attention and decide what I might do differently in the future based on what I have learned.

There are many ways to approach the reading of a new book. This is only the one I choose. I invite you try the ideas that interest you and see what you think. Develop your own mental model for reading books and above all enjoy.

My library continues to grow as I select books I want to keep and reread or return to.

It is fun to reread book years later and see how what interests me has changed.

Journaling

L ike most children, I was given or started numerous diaries. They lasted about two weeks before being buried beneath the debris that was my desk. Mostly they were single lines about something I did that day ala rode my bike to school today.

The first journal that I stayed with came when I was in college. I was in a health class as I recall and we were talking about fatigue. I had opened my journal and was giving it a title. I wrote "Creative" and then allowed the ambiance of the class discussion to lead me to add "fatigue". I looked at that and decided to accept it. So the title of my journals for many years thereafter was "Creative Fatigue". The title seemed to evoke my life at that time – a balance between creativity and the fatigue of long college days of study and learning.

The blank books I started as a child were always called diaries. Why then was I now calling this a journal? For me, a diary is something you write in every day and so if I did not write in my diary every day I had failed. But a journal could be written when I wanted to – once a week, several times in a day or even with a hiatus of a year or two.

A journal is one of those things that work for me. I am now writing in my 45th journal and have written journals for 55 years. And so what will become of all of these journals? If you decide to try journaling, that will be up to you. Some feel a need to hide them and protect them. Some want them burned at their death. My children do not seem to want them.

So, over time, I have decided that I want my journals saved. I have decided to donate them to my alma mater. As such, I now include current event articles in my journals. It gives them a timeframe that I hope will be interesting to future readers.

On the other hand, I wish I had the journals of my grandparents or great grandparents.

I once belonged to a journal reading group. We read and discussed journals of famous people and "How to" journals. We learned and laughed and made friends.

Perhaps my effort at privacy is my poor handwriting. Future readers will need to decipher certain parts of my writing or hope to understand from context. And if our children stop learning cursive, they may need to rely on future computer technology to read it at all.

So, what does this all lead to? Journaling is a "mental model" I have found useful. I use my journal to set goals, to evaluate, to express feelings, to collect ideas, etc. So, try journaling. If you like it, keep doing it and change it over time to meet your needs. Make it a routine, a mental model that makes your days better, happier, more balanced, more creative.

I now keep several journals: a book journal, a Happy journal, a gardening journal, a travel journal, etc. Think about journals you might like to try. And above all, have fun.

Journal Frontispieces

I nside the cover of each journal is a list of yearly goals set to these categories: creative, emotional, financial, physical, spiritual and mental. I check these off as I complete them or cross them off when they no longer seem relevant. From these I plan monthly goals and at the end of the month record monthly successes. Since savoring our successes so often gets neglected, this helps me remember that I am accomplishing, even as the "to do" list continues to expand.

Next I draw a shield and a motto. I decide on a motto for the year and put that on a banner across the shield. There are four sections to the shield: what I want to be remembered for, three wishes if I knew I could not fail, my three greatest accomplishments and three things others can do for me.

Then I define my purpose and a successful day. I list my values and my talents. And proclaim a vision for the time period of this particular journal (usually about a year).

I few years ago, I learned about making Vision Maps in the form of a collage. So, I collect pictures and words (perhaps photographs or a poem I have written and sit down to design a cover for my journal. I glue the pieces in place and then cover them with clear contact paper. It makes a nice visual of where I am and where I am going.

Autobiographical Vignettes

E very once in a while, I think that I would like to start writing my
autobiography. But if I manage to put pen to paper, I generally
get about one to three pages done before I put it aside and manage
to forget to come back to it.

So, I was impressed by an instructor who suggested that we all
find it easier to write stories than to take on such a major task. He
suggested that we write our stories, the little scenarios that stir our
memories, the lessons we have learned along the way, the people we
have interacted with. And so, I began.

I now have two thick volumes of stories and poetry. I have even
found it necessary to break my stories down into categories. My
vignettes are now divided into:

Stories that introduce me

Stories of my ancestry

Stories of when I was a child

Stories of raising my own family

Stories of life after all of my children have left home

Stories about the entirety of my life

Political Commentary

Ponderings

When I first started writing these stories I thought it would be
great to share them with my children, so at Christmas I would put
together a folder of all the stories I had written that year and send

them out. I soon learned that they were not always appreciated. Each of us sees the same experiences differently.

Since this was about the time that "The World According to Garp" came out, I added a front page that said "The World According to Barbara" and invited them to rewrite the stories according to their recollections. None of them ever did.

Perhaps my children will never appreciate these stories, but their children or their grandchildren surely will. So I keep writing.

Are there stories in your life that need to be written down before they are forgotten? See if this resonates with you. Give it a try.

Health Journal

How many times have you been in a doctor's office when he asked when did you get your last tetanus shot and you sit there trying to think back and figure out when and where? As I get older it gets harder and harder to remember.

So, several years ago, I decided that I needed to keep better records and have them available when I am at the doctor's office. I started a small journal, small enough to carry easily when I visit the doctor.

First, I put the current date on the first page. But then I did a retrospective look back at all I could remember of my life as it came to health problems or doctor visits. Then I asked close relatives what they remembered. With a good background, I then started with the current date to record doctor visits, diagnoses and included my weight and blood pressure. Now I have an ongoing record.

Next I turned to the back of the book and made a chart of all vaccinations and inoculations. Another page recorded all hospitalizations and surgeries. Still another was for accidents. You can add whatever else seems pertinent. This little book makes such a difference in my doctor visits and the health staff really appreciates this little book. In addition, I carry a list of all of the medications that I take. Including the non-prescription ones, so doctors can be aware of possible interactions and let me know about them.

I also keep a second health journal that is filled with ideas, menus and suggestions for improving my health. Then when I am wondering what to do about itching, I know there are several tips available for my perusal.

These are a couple of ideas that work for me. What might work for you and how would you like to arrange them? Be willing to try something and to change it as you come up with something better. Then share the ideas that work particularly well with others and gather their ideas as well to improve what you are doing and what you would like to do.

Compliments

Have you ever noticed how a compliment seems to fly by almost unnoticed and often unremembered, but a criticism lodges firmly to worry and nag at you?

I have learned to work at capturing those compliments. First, really hear them. Take them in. No inner critic rebuttals allowed. No denigration. Breathe deeply. Acknowledge with a simple "thank-you". No, you do not need to come up with an immediate return compliment either.

Then write down the compliment. I keep an ongoing list in the back of my journal.

Then, when a day comes that everything is not going so well, I go to the journal and again appreciate what others have said about me. I smile and take it all in. You might be surprised how this list can raise you spirits.

Now is a good time to think about the ones who gave them and perhaps pen a note thanking them for all of whom they are.

You could also put each one in a jar and then draw one out to read when you are feeling low. This is your mental model. Use it in whatever way produces the best results for you.

I can almost see your smile, even now.

Harvesting Your Journals

Journals are a great resource for gifts. When my granddaughter, Heather, was approaching her tenth birthday, I wanted something different for her birthday. First, I wrote a poem for her and then went back through my journals to see what I had written the year her mother was ten. I made a small booklet for Heather that told all about the things her mother said and did when she was ten.

That was the beginning of a new family activity. When my son announced his engagement, I started putting together a book for his bride with baby pictures of him, a family tree and stories and poems of his life and growth. It was a favorite gift and every child since then has wanted the same personalized gift.

Computers make this an easier job with publication software and I go to the local printer for colored covers and binding. With time I have learned to make a second copy to keep for myself. Have you ever made something nice, given it away and later wished you had one as well? The books tell us to love ourselves first. So, make a gift for yourself as well.

The ideas are limitless. Your creativity gets a place to expand and fill with possibilities and you leave a piece of yourself in many homes and lives.

The only warning is "beware of expectations". After one or two, it is easy to expect "nice words". They do not always come. Your joy must come from the creativity and the joy of the project itself.

Someone will say "that's not the way I remember it". And it is not, for our memories are seen through our own eyes and tinted with our own backgrounds. That comment could spark a great conversation that warms hearts with even more memories, more opportunities to reminisce, to connect, to laugh and enjoy each other.

Tidbits

When reading directions or warranties, read all of the details. It is easy to get the idea and think you know all you need to know. But it only takes a moment to read all the way through and perhaps find a line that changes everything. Take the time and read it all.

When talking to someone and a great idea that you want to follow up on comes up, put it in writing. We always think we will remember more than we do. So carry a small notebook and a pen with you all the time or speak it into your smart phone.

Keep an envelope in your car and put all receipts in it. You never know when you will need one and are glad you have it. Go through them and get rid of the ones you will no longer need at the end of each month.

When you appreciate someone, tell them.

Always hike or swim with a buddy. This is one of those lessons you learn in a Scouting program. A corollary is: don't go on a trip without leaving a friend with an itinerary and a planned date of return. That way if something happens or someone needs to reach you there is a place to start in trying to locate you.

A PLACE FOR YOU TO ADD YOUR OWN "AHA'S"

Printed in the United States
By Bookmasters